TRIUMPH HOUSE
Poetry with a Purpose

SILENT VOICES

Edited by

CHRIS WALTON

First published in Great Britain in 1998 by
TRIUMPH HOUSE
1-2 Wainman Road, Woodston,
Peterborough, PE2 7BU
Telephone (01733) 230749

HB ISBN 1 86161 304 0
SB ISBN 1 86161 309 1

FOREWORD

Hearing Dogs for Deaf People is a registered charity which selects and trains dogs, most of them from rescue centres, to alert their deaf owners to sounds which hearing people often take for granted, such as the alarm clock, doorbell, telephone and smoke alarm. The practical value is obvious but the therapeutic value should not be underestimated as among reported benefits, many recipients also find substantially increased confidence and independence.

Since the charity began in 1982, many hearing dog recipients have written lovely stories, poems and even books about their four-legged companions so it is a wonderful opportunity to be able to put together an anthology of a selection of these poems. However, it is not just the recipients whose hearts are touched by these very special dogs and many of our volunteers have also been inspired to put pen to paper.

Most of the 130 poems included are about dogs but there are also quite a few about deafness which, after all, is why *Hearing Dogs for Deaf People* was set up in the first place.

I do hope you enjoy reading this book. As our charity benefits from the sale of each book, buying a copy of 'Silent Voices' is another way to help us train more dogs for deaf people - thank you.

A G Blunt
Director General
Hearing Dogs for Deaf People

CONTENTS

Norma's Ears

Didi was confused by something he'd overheard
A cat was talking about him
'He's like a pair of ears!' she purred
Now Didi loved his mistress
Norma was the name
He never left her side
You see she like to play a game
Didi had to make a fuss whenever he heard a noise
And if he did it properly
He'd get hugs and treats and toys
But when Didi looked at Norma's ears, small and
                                    fleshy and pink
He remembered what the cat had said
It did half make him think!
He was a dog, white and fluffy
Not at all like a pair of ears
If he thought he looked all pink and flappy
                    his day would end in tears
But Didi had another thought which made
                            him smile instead
How funny his mistress Norma would look
With a dog on each side of her head!

Wendy J Turner

UNTITLED

If I could not hear I would miss the sound of :

> The soft rain dripping on the house tops.
> Oceans swishing around.
> The wind singing to me.
> Trees swishing around and around.
> My best friend's voice.
> Birds singing in the morning.

Ashley Taylor (7)

UNTITLED

If I could not hear I would miss

> The sound of my mum's voice.
> When a car alarm goes off.
> When my fire alarm goes off.
> The leaves falling.
> The trees blowing.
> When my friend sings.
> A dog barking.

Joshua Frayne (7)

MAN'S BEST FRIEND

He cheers us up when we feel sad.
He plays with us when we are bored.
He jumps at me when I come home from school.
Man's best friend
He comes to me when I'm watching TV
He licks my hand.
He jumps at me when I am eating my tea.
Man's best friend.

Annabelle Keegan (7)

UNTITLED

If I could not hear
I would miss the sound of

> A bird singing in my back garden.
> My mum's voice.
> My house alarm.
> A bird in my tree in my back garden.
> The trees whistling.
> My dad's voice.
> A dog barking.
> I will miss the wind blowing
> > in the air.

Michaela Drew (7)

UNTITLED

If I could not hear
I would miss the sound of

> The waves at sea.
> Animals in the countryside.
> The air blowing with the clouds in the sky.
> The leaves shaking.
> The school singing
> The flowers blowing.
> The children laughing.
> The parrots squawking at the zoo.

Lois Pendleton (7)

UNTITLED

If I could not hear
I would miss the sound of

My teacher speaking
The sound of Oscar barking
The music of the Spice Girls
The sound of the little people singing
My Tamagochi beeping
The smoke alarm
My brother reading.

Jade Sullivan (7)

UNTITLED

If I could not hear
I would miss the sound of

> My mum speaking softly to me
> My favourite programme
> My best friend's voice
> The school singing
> My sister saying funny words to me
> When I'm playing 'tag' and I'm not 'it'.
> The white snow falling softly and slowly
> The bells of Father Christmas.

Stacey Cowan (7)

A HEARING DOG ALPHABET

A	he's attentive and assuring
B	my best friend, and better than any electrical aids
C	imparting confidence, he's calming when I've had a chaotic day
D	devoted and dependable
E	he's energetic and engaging - he's my *ears*
F	a spur to fitness and fulfilment, faithful, of course
G	he guards my safety night and day
H	helps my daily living
I	investigative, intelligent, indispensable
J	he brings joy into my life
K	kindness is all he asks for in return
L	lively, he listens when I talk to him and understands me, signing too.
M	I'm his mum and he loves me, could I ask for more?
N	naughty - never! (well, rarely ever)
O	obviously obedient
P	patient and playful, a positive plus for me
Q	qualifications guaranteed by undaunted untiring, sympathetic trainers
R	reliable - he responds to bells and alarms I cannot hear
S	supportive - 'He's a Star,' did you say - well that's his name
T	his touch tells me when I'm needed - he's a talking point with others that I meet.
U	united, we're a team, undeterred by unexpected situations
V	valued for the A-Z here listed, volunteers when help is needed
W	working dog of the highest degree he's a WAG not a PhD
X	extraordinary example of the care and the compassion exemplified at Lewknor and at York
Y	yappie - emphatically *No!* Hearing Dogs do not offend Touch is that upon which they depend
Z	zealous, with appeal, he zaps into action, attracts my attention

A-Z, Z-A . . . conclusion - my dog really is a chum
Thank you for the charity where so many hearts are won.

Caroline Gambell

RUTH

Dear Ruth,

    Now you're here to stay
I appreciate you more each day.
With a wag of your tail,
You say 'Hello,'
You became my ears,
Allay! All my fears,
Of other pals I've quite a few,
None dear Ruth to equal you.

Kay Stafford

CONSPIRACY OF SILENCE

People pass like ships in the night,
I am an island in a sea of faces.
In a room, the talk is an undulating current
That rises and falls around me.
I am alone, lost and drowning
In the grumble and the mumble of sound.

My hearing (or the lack of it) blurs the world around
While the normal people continue with their talk.
They all look at each other, smiling and speaking,
Lit from within by the warmth of communication.
I sit frozen and forgotten, corpse-like in the corner:
How often they lock me out of their lives.

I am a non-person. I never happened.
Why do they not acknowledge me,
Raise their voices above the humdrum so I can hear?
I fade to grey before their eyes, numb and alone and petrified.
They have no patience: I would ask them to repeat,
But it is like King Canute telling the waves to turn back.

David Tallach

HE KNOWS EXACTLY WHAT TO DO

I may be deaf but I can feel,
And I can see the urgency that's real
When my new friend paws at my knee
With *important message* just for me.
Eyes left, eyes left, with tail that's wagging hard and fast -
I think I understand at last,
There's someone knocking at my door.
Quick, follow Friend across the floor!

Duty done, it's back to bed
To rest his little weary head.
He's my new *ears,* all radar-tuned to serve my special needs
So that I can follow where he leads.
He knows exactly what to do.
He's been trained to guide me through
My silent world, alerting me to urgent sound,
Using body language in every way that can be found.

I wake to find him on my knee,
All soft and warm and dozing peacefully.
The kettle's boiled - it's time for tea.
He taps me twice upon the knee
And heads towards the kitchen door.
His reward's a biscuit on the floor.
We share a cup of tea or two.
Oh yes, he knows just what to do -
He's my new *ears*, you see,
A link through him from you to me.

Eileen M Lodge

BEE

As a pup she was not thin
But squashy, black and round,
Now she keeps herself in trim
Ten inches off the ground.

Cares in the world she has not got
(Nothing bothers her a lot)
Daddy's girl she has become
And everything she does for fun.

Claire Guest & Andrew Cook

HONEY

I'm no champ, I'm a scamp
A brat, a spoilt pup
Despite my exalted lineage
I'm in no way stuck up.

I'm a normal healthy dog
Who likes to run and play
Not be placed on a pedestal
Admired by humans, night and day.

I should have long flowing locks
With an arrogant pose
I have short curly hair
and a turned up nose.

Those long flowing locks
I just could not keep clean
The beautician she clipped me
The results you have seen.

My people think I'm perfect
As is right and proper you know.
They brushed me and groomed me
For Belturbet Dog Show.

The judge looked at me
The judge said 'What is that?'
This show is for dogs
You have entered a cat!

I'm a Tibetan Lion Dog
Worth a lot more than money
A pedigree Shih Tzu
An aristocrat called Honey.

Catherine Brady

DEAFNESS AND BLINDNESS

Deafness is a world of silence,
Deafness is a world of misery,
Deafness is an unseen disability,
Deafness is a world of sadness,
Deafness is being laughed at
        when you communicate.

Without sight you couldn't see,
Without sight you couldn't picture
        or shape simple items,
Without sight you couldn't do things by yourself,
Without sight you wouldn't know if people
        were laughing at you,
Without sight life is worthless.

Imagine being Deaf and Blind,
No sight,
No hearing,
No form of communication, and worst of all
Not knowing that you exist.

Lee Kelly

IF I COULD NOT HEAR

If I could not hear
I would miss the sound of

> The laughter of children on the beach
> Birds singing in the garden
> Music playing softly
> A loud fire alarm
> A dog barking
> and water running.

Rose Dindol (7)

IF I COULD NOT HEAR

If I could not hear
I would miss the sound of

> Singing at daylight
> Nice gentle music on the radio
> Leaves making crunchy noises
> My friend using a nice gentle voice
> The sea making a nice 'wave' sound
> People playing the drums gently
> The hailstones tapping on the roof.

Andrew Crook (7)

LIMERICK

There was a young dog called O'Leary
Whose eyesight was ever so bleary
He chased after a buck
And in a hole got stuck
Chasing rabbits is okay in theory!

Cllla Bllgh

A GIFT TO TREASURE

I can't imagine only guess
What it's like to be deaf,
Not to be able to hear a thing
The wind, rain, or the birds sing
Or the rustling of leaves
And the sounds of the seas,
I would miss these wonderful sounds
Only in nature can they be found.
Most of us take our hearing for granted
Always hearing every word that is said,
Some people haven't heard for years
A hearing aid can help them to hear
But not give them back normal hearing
And there is sign language they can be learning,
The way to help others who cannot hear
Is to look at them and stand near
Your face they should be able to see
Talk to them slowly and clearly
We live in a world that is full of noise
And to those of us who can hear - it annoys
Like when we are trying to sleep at night
Then we long for some peace and quiet,
We should treasure the gift of hearing
And be grateful if we can hear everything.

Linda Roberts

TO A FRIEND WHO IS COMPLETELY DEAF

I give thanks to God, that I have my hearing
which gives me independence
without which I would feel resentment
and nervous at all times, upon living alone
that at night I would not hear
if thieves entered my home
putting me in danger of attack
while at the same time stealing a sack
of the few valuables I have accrued
bring memories back, some of which I rued.
I'd fear being alone in my world of silence
People would get frustrated with me,
bringing tears to my eye, making me want to cry,
If only I had a hearing dog, to take me out of this fog
but being dependant on the state, I could only hope and wait
that monies would be raised to help train a dog who'd be my mate
who would let me know if the doorbell rings, and this would bring
new meaning to my life, ending the strife and at the same time
my loneliness, with my new friend Bess
no longer would I be isolated and alone
but would have the company of Bess while she chewed her bone
contented and at rest, with me alone.

Maureen Eccles

A LOYAL FRIEND

You don't have to look far for a friend.
Just visit a rescue animal pen.
There are all types of dogs you will find
Looking for someone loving and kind.

There will be dogs large and small
Waiting for the right person to call
To take them to their home
So they will never more roam.

Once that dog has settled down
Love and faithfulness will be found.
When a cold nose snuggles up to you
You will know it was the right thing to do.

The love a dog gives is hard to find
But I know you will feel peace of mind.
Knowing you have given it a place
To sleep by your fireplace.

I had my dog for seventeen years.
She comforted me through joy and tears.
She is no longer here with me,
But her memory will always be.

Jean Bradbury

CHOOSING A DOG FOR LIFE

So . . . you want to buy a puppy . . . well here's a rough guide
Remember . . . for a lifetime he'll be by your side
And for his mum the first night he'll be crying
For everyone at home this will be trying . . .

As a pup over his actions he has no control
He'll make himself sick gobbling all sorts of things whole
He's full of energy when you are feeling frail
and just guard your precious things when he wags his tail . . .

Why not a house-trained dog from a sanctuary get
Home a retired greyhound . . . a gentle quiet pet
If you are a rambler or really need to trim
how about an Afghan hound . . . you'll walk miles with him

Or old English sheepdog (Dulux) with big feet
(Did you know their hair can be spun like wool of sheep)
The Welsh corgi can be a bit nippy they say
Jack Russells are fun and always ready to play

The boxer too seems a happy sort of chap
and the little Yorkies just fit on the lap.
There are wee Chihuahuas and big-boned Alsations
Low slung Basset hounds and spotted Dalmations

So this list of dogs can go on and on
Some need hours of grooming with coats that hang long
In temperament they can be zany, fierce or kind
So consider well before you make up your mind.

Finally . . . you've seen dogs that take owners for the walk
These dogs are in charge . . . they've no need to talk!
Which of you will be the boss . . . your dog needs to know
So . . . off to dog-training classes . . . *you both must go!*

Valerie Ovais

BE OPENED!

'Ephata!' He said - 'Be opened!' And the man could hear.
Lord . . . that sounds so clear and simple. Yes, for You were there.
You could make the deaf to listen, hearts to leap with joy,
Tongues once mute, to speak a language, souls and bodies whole.
Work on me, then, in Your mercy. Hear my cry for help!
I am deaf and dumb, too often, closed upon myself,
Hearing not the people around me, for I do not care:
Grasping not the signs you send me, ignoring Your words.
Listening not, I cannot hear - and so, I cannot speak.
Open wide our hearts at last, Lord, to receive . . . then give.

Katharine Holmstrom

MY FRIEND

I have a friend
I love so dear
He gives me hope
He gives me care
]
At night we sit alone
He chews on a bone
Till the time for bed
Up the stairs he fled.

My company
My help
My best friend
My dog.

Pat Sunderland

THE JOYS OF HEARING

To live in a world that is silent
With ne'er an affectionate word,
A whisper of comfort when needed,
Where musical notes are not heard,

Is missing the joys of the hearing,
The song of the lark at the dawn,
The drone of the bees in the heather,
The laugh of a child on the lawn.

The fanfare of trumpets so striking,
An alphorn's rich sound on the heights,
The cry of a seagull in passing,
The hooting of owls in the nights.

The soar of sopranos in chorus,
The silvery tones of a bell,
The waves of the sea as they're breaking,
The whisper of trees in the dell.

Oh, may those with hearing be grateful
And not take for granted that they
Are able to hear all the sounds in the air
That are all around us each day.

Joyce M Turner

MAN'S BEST FRIEND

He cheers us up when
we feel sad.
He comes to you.
He plays with you
Man's best friend!

Alex Bilton (6)

UNTITLED

If I could not hear
I would miss the sound

      Of my music.
      My fire alarm.
      My cat alarm.
      My best friend's voice
      The sound of birds singing
                at daylight.
      My mum's voice.
      The leaves falling.
      The trees blowing.

Vanessa Sturman (7)

OBSESSION

I'm obsessed and can talk of nothing else
But my new love
His bearing is regal, he stands tall and erect
His legs are firm and strong
And his lips soft and gentle

My new love and I pass many an hour
Just being ourselves
Speaking without words, because we understand
He kisses my hand, the new man in my life -
My dog.

Dorothy Tarleton

JUBILANT JUNO

My choice dog jaunt in Snowdonia
Is from Beddgelert to the peak.
I enjoy the scent of Erica,
I bark a lot but cannot speak.

The village legend of Gelert's grave,
Slain by the Prince whose child was killed
By wolf destroyed by this dog so brave,
Makes man's best friend forever thrilled.

As Juno wire-haired fox terrier,
Each day I race around the field.
In rain nothing could be merrier
With umbrella for a shield.

I lie down and wait with TV on,
Closing my ears and eyes in sleep.
I dream of rabbits, watch how they run,
Hearing their incredible bleep.

No watch or alarm I know the time,
When to get up and wake master.
Stretching my legs, up the stairs I climb;
Downstairs what tasty provender.

Ever on guard, alert to all sounds
I growl, to stop any alien;
Then deaf friends, from their silence rebound,
Call me, for speed, Watchdog Champion.

It's grand to live in the countryside,
Rushing through wood and waterway.
Free to walk from morn to eventide,
Then snug in homely hideaway.

Jeanette Fairclough

DOES HE LAUGH?

These people sneer at our belief,
They mock the sacred. Like a thief
They take our precious, holy things
And twist and turn them into slings
To throw at us crude blasphemy,
(One time accounted infamy)
To shrieks of laughter from the dolts
Whose mirth a thoughtful mind revolts:
So very great 'Humanity'!
They need not God, for verily
They do more miracles than He!
Put probes on Mars; through concrete see;
Play games with genes - and don't forget
They've even made the Internet!
But is this new? John the Divine
Saw this in dream of Palestine!
Two witnesses to God most High
Speak in Jerusalem - and die.
All peoples, tongues and nations see
Their bodies lie there. Can this be?
Oh yes! They'll see them without doubt,
On 'News at Ten' or thereabout
And on a sudden, sage or scout
Around the world, hear Trump or Shout
When God in judgement rides the skies.
He'll use their Internet! Surprise?

Elsie Norman

INDEPENDENCE

I know that in life
We all strive for
Independence from
Such a young age
We take it for granted
A process of growing
It shows in a number of ways
We can hear every sound
That is uttered
From laughter a bird
Many things
But it would be
So hard to imagine
A silent world
Deafness can bring
Could we do more
To give independence
Where people could go
Where they choose
With a dog to hear
And form a friendship
They have gained
We have nothing to lose.

Jeanette Gaffney

SHE WHO MUST BE OBEYED

A gentle nudge upon my arm, given by a small paw,
And then she shepherds me along, quickly to the door.
To where awaits the postman perhaps, maybe, a friend.
I look at her with gratitude as on our way we wend.

What could I do without her? To live here all alone.
My helper and companion, who brightens up my home.
I cannot hear a phone bell ring, and sometimes miss its light.

That's when she scampers up to me, makes everything alright
For with the visual telephone I can take the call,
It really brightens up my day. To her I owe it all.

Wakes me in the morning. Can tell when something falls,
Warns me, so I am prepared, when the vicar calls.
So many things she does for me, I bless the day she came,
For I know that without her, it could never be the same.

And when she sits upon my lap, we talk in our own way,
Her eyes, the turning of her head, have so much more to say
Than any bright young chatterbox of tender years, maybe.
The wagging tail, the knowing look, the love she gives to me.

Her gentle ways beguile my heart, and seem to calm my fears
She is my servant - boss - and friend, much more than that

my *ears!*

I thank God for His blessing, for I know that I am blest
To have a dog like *Sheba* to bring such happiness.

Dennis Brockelbank

A MOST TREASURED PET

Once upon a time there was a pup named Bingo.
He was happy at home, and soon learned the lingo
Of 'Walk,' 'Sit,' 'Fetch,' 'Down boy' and 'Stay.'
He was bright as a button and learned more each day.

His owners loved him and held him a creature most dear -
But, both out at work, lead them to fear
That young Bingo was bored, too much time on his own -
He was one year old now and quite fully grown.

A friend when apprised of the problem in hand
Said she had heard an appeal broadcast over the land -
By an organisation - *Hearing Dogs for Deaf People.*
she wondered if Bingo for this task was suitable?

His owners rang up the phone number given
And Bingo to office for assessment was driven.
'He's as bright as a button' his owners repeated
To the official when all were comfortably seated.

Bingo obeyed and performed all his tricks
The official, impressed, described how things were fixed
For Bingo to learn to be the *new ears*
Of someone who was deaf, quite unable to hear.

Dear reader, to cut a long story short,
Bingo was happy to be expertly taught,
When bells, alarms, door knockers sound,
To attract the attention of the new friend he's found.

His old owners are proud of the young dog their ex-pet.
His deaf master's new ears he's become and has met
With his purpose in life for many years yet.
We all know he'll be happy - *a most treasured pet.*

M C Cobb

HEARING DOGS FOR THE DEAF

If you call upon someone,
Who really cannot hear,
Unless they can see you,
They won't know you're anywhere near.

But that today
May not always be the case
They may have a very dear friend
With a distinctive canine face.

For dogs, are now trained,
to hear the phone; or doorbell too,
And so lead their owner,
So they, can answer you.

The alarm goes in the morning,
To get them out of bed.
But it's only the alerted dog
Who will tell them what is said -
That it's time to rise;
To start another day,
Not forgetting their little dog,
For helping them on their way.

It takes endless work and patience
To react in such a way,
But, all so rewarding
To help someone else's day.

P Saw

THE SILENT WISDOM OF LOVE

When sadness filled the world for me
By 'Shimmer's' death I wept quite openly.
Her help beside me as I spoke.
In aid of Hearing Dogs gave hope.
To all of those who could not hear,
By seeing her. Learnt help was near.

Then 'Lindsay' came to carry on,
The noble work she had begun.
By 'Shimmer' in those far-off days
To help fund-raising in many ways.
With touch of paw, she'll quietly tell,
That someone's rung the front door bell.
Her gentle and most loving nature,
As she works with me is quite a feature.
So once again with her support,
How proud I am to do my work.
To tell all those with hard of hearing
That now they have a new beginning
In life so wondrous with their friend,
A 'Hearing Dog' right to the end.

Ambi Jamison

NOT SUCH A DUMB FRIEND'S DAY

It's a yawn at dawn when the alarm clock rings
and the postman knocks and the kettle sings,
Then, when we walk, I hear the sounds
with which the outside world abounds
but my 'boss' can't know what's going on
it's *my* ears that she relies upon.

I tell her all she needs to know
to keep her safe, for where we go
I warn of dangers she can't hear
And help avoid the lurking fear
of things outside her field of vision
but which *I hear* as soon as they've arisen.

Back home in 'peaceful domesticity' (!)
all things powered by E-lectricity
all 'peep' and 'squeak' from time to time
and then responsibility is mine
to tell the missus what and when
needs switching off and on again.

When there's a ringing telephone
I don't have time to chew my bone
it's a dash to tell her there's a call
so she can take it in the hall,
and switch it to her message taker
the amazing sounds-to-words translator!

Knocks on door and ringing bell,
all kinds of sounds I sort and tell
and in particular the smoke alarm
keeps my ears alert and my boss from harm,
so with paws and leaps and signals taught
I make her days a lot less fraught.

What else? Oh yes! And apart from 'hearing'
I believe she finds me quite endearing -
it's mutual I am pleased to say,
so we play and cuddle every day!
She may be deaf - and of course I'm 'dumb'
but she loves me - and to me she's Mum!

When it's time to go to bed
I rest and think within my head
How *silent* must my Mum's world be!
How *would* she cope without her 'little me'?
- 'Cos it's all that love and all that sharing
that's so rewarding, warm and caring.

Colin R Paine

MY SPECIAL FRIEND

I have a little friend,
really special to me.
He has four legs and one wet nose
And I feel he's set me free.
At last I can be myself,
and live a life that's mine
And I know he'll help me through
With not a bark or whine.
But touch and tell, which is his way
To make me understand.
He wakes me up, we share our days
I love my little friend.

Laureen Sykes

TO BE DEAF

To be deaf
Must be bereft.
Never to hear the birds
singing in the bough.
Never to hear a cat's
plaintive 'meow',
Never to hear the wind
rushing through the tree.
Never to hear my friend
calling after me.
Never to hear the waves
crash on the seashore,
Never to hear my grandsons
tapping on the door.
Never to hear them laughing
and calling out 'Grandma!
Never to hear them shout
Hip, hip, hoorah!
Never to hear on the radio
that old-tyme favourite song.
Always to live in a silent world
Oh, how would I keep strong?
To be deaf
must be bereft.

Maisie Dance

PUPPY'S WALK

Come along puppy, before it gets dark,
We're going for a walk, down the road to the park.
We might meet your doggy friends, both big and small,
And have a fun-filled game with a ball.

But when you grow up, cuddly, cute little boy,
You'll do something greater than play with a toy.
For you, my puppy dog, in future years,
Will hopefully act as a deaf person's ears.

Margaret Conrad

EARS

My name is Ears or maybe not,
As I'm the deafest of the lot.
I run around and play all day,
Trying to hear what people say.
All my friends can hear a lot,
But I cannot as I'm the deafest
                           of the lot.

Laura Anderson (10)

SHEBA THE GANNET

Sheba is my big black dog,
But she eats more like a horse.
She's old and fat and nearly blind,
But we all still love her, of course.

She reckons that she's deaf when
                 you call her to come,
For a bath or a pill or a spray.
But open a sweet or a packet of crisps,
And watch out if you get in her way.

Call of a cat and she'll come instead,
If she thinks that she will miss out.
If food is on her mind (which it always is),
You don't even have to shout.

Just pick up a tin or open a pack,
And the sound will bring her straight there.
Just rattle the dish and call the cat,
And she'll appear from who-knows-where.

She sleeps all day (on my bed of course),
She just wakes up to eat.
But we all love her just the same,
And her love for us can't be beat.

S Williams

A RAY OF HOPE

*(For my gran who is deaf and her
hearing dog Laura)*

A silent world where nothing's clear,
a scary place when you can't hear,
How hard it is to make a stand when you can hardly
understand.

Then suddenly a ray of hope appears, and this ray of
hope has hearing ears.
A dog that will erase all fears
And give you lots of love.

Rebecca Gooden

A LOT OF FAITH

Yes I have a lot of faith
In all the people around me
For they are soon there when I need them
Right there standing by my knee.

And I have a lot of hope
For when I am getting old
For my faith will pull me through
Without ever having to be told.

So I have a lot of charity
With those who appear to care for me
For I will bring them anything
Even the world you see.

Keith L Powell

YOU ARE GONE

You're gone old lad - can it be true?
Fresh fields - you've left to roam
While I am left with an longing ache
Sobbing and so alone.
I see your faithful trusting eyes
As you wearily looked to me
Saying 'You know best - and I'm so tired'
Then your head sunk down on my knee
I knew then - that your time had come
And I couldn't prolong your fight
I cuddled you close - gave a nod to the vet
Then tears were blurring my sight
So ended weeks of hopes and prayers
So came the worst of my fears
You were off to a happier hunting ground
I was left behind with my tears
And as I came to realise - that you would never wake
I sobbed alone and thought - old lad
My heart must surely break
You were off to a place where dogs run free
Amid winding paths - tree-lined
And you'll never know - old pal of mine
The heartbreak you leave behind
I loved you so - you see old lad
I could not watch your pain
But I know that I can never love -
A dog that way again
You gave so much - my faithful Shep
While the trust from your soft eyes shone.
With tear-dimmed ones I am forced to admit
You're gone old lad . . . *you're gone!*

Irene Beattie

UNTITLED

If I could not hear I would miss
the sound of

> Favourite music that went loud and soft.
> My best friend singing a beautiful song.
> Beautiful leaves crackling.
> Morning birds singing,
> Your favourite film.

You wouldn't hear
> The door bell ringing

You wouldn't hear
> the telephone ringing, or
> Wedding bells ringing.

Jessica Roberts (6)

LOVE ME ENOUGH

(Dedicated to Charlie who
died April 7th, 1992
He holds my heart)

My eyes grow dim and weary
It really is too tough.
Not to the vet's again, Mum,
Please love me enough.

Love me enough when the time comes
When there's no more a vet can do.
Love me enough to let me go
Yes, I know you suffer too.

I'm sorry I won't be with you
This time, to lick your tears.
But think of all the joy, Mum,
We've shared throughout the years.

Stay with me please, I ask you
'Til the vet's injection works.
Please hold me as you let me go,
For it hurts me to leave, I love you so.

I feel your tears on my fur, Mum,
But it has to be this way.
Please give some other a home, Mum,
For I can no longer stay.

My Lord, it hurts as I leave her
To see her crying so

         I'm drifting and I'm free now
         As from the body's pain I go.

    *   *   *   *   *   *   *

Little puppy snoozing in your Mother's paws,
Listen as I whisper so no one else can hear,
When you awake you'll see her,

That woman - over there!
Wag your tail, go to her, she is the one for you.
Care for her and love her,
That's all you need to do.

I see them walk together where with her I used to go,
She smiles gently as I touch her, she feels my warm embrace

> For I am in the soft wind
> That quietly kisses her face.

Anita Richards

LIFE WITH BEN

I needed independence,
I'd found a little flat.
My parents were against it,
'You cannot live like that.

'You'll never hear the telephone'
'What if someone calls?'
'Life will be so silent,
Within these four small walls.'

But I was quite determined,
I'd make it in the end.
Because I had planned to meet,
A very special friend.

His eyes are brown, his paws are large,
He gently licks my hands.
He's trained to listen in for me,
This he understands.

His name is Ben, he'll be with me,
For many, many years.
I thank the Lord for sending him,
For lending me his ears.

I also bless the trainers,
For their patience and their care.
Thanks and congratulations,
From deaf folk everywhere.

Peggy Howe

FROM SILENCE SET FREE

Sounds the deaf cannot hear,
Make Lucky run and paw my leg;
The door bell chimes out clear,
The phone rings, call from Winnipeg.
That touch makes me ask, what is it?
Follow her lead, surprise visit.

Off we go, morning jaunt,
On bridle paths to open field;
The fan-shaped palm leaves flaunt;
The quiet copse with hillside shield,
Glistens with dew, freshens the turf,
Wing-beat of seagulls dive to surf,

Super days together,
Bonding closely in harmony,
Romping across heather,
Merry, frolicsome company.
Ours the whole green valley this way,
Country scents, loyalty's heyday.

From sphere of quietness,
We enter a firm partnership;
Open gates to gladness,
On tracks leading to comradeship.
Beyond all sinister shadows,
To fresh rollicking calypsos.

Around us beauty lies,
Trees make sounds Lucky's ears can catch;
I watch her sparkling eyes,
Excited like a football match.
Voiceless she gives her secret clue,
Of rural delights ever new.

Hearing dogs are sounds seen.
Their lightest touch speaks in silence;
Each act a go-between,
From stillness to significance.
Noisiness drowns loving whispers,
Guide dogs living language leaders!

James Leonard Clough

MY WONDERFUL DOGS
(For Lady, Tommy, Oliver, Pepe and Joe)

My dogs like playing in summer sun,
like puppies o'er the grass they run,
in the air they leap with barking sound,
like children they tumble to the ground,
wind sweeps through their soothing coat,
to frolic they would each day devote!

In restless, passionate joy they whirl,
pirouetting dancers, they skilfully swirl,
darting and twisting in needles of light,
dogs at play such a wonderful sight,
chasing tails, going round and round,
what faithful friends I have found!

Intelligent, loving, with sparkling eyes,
reliable, patient, understanding and wise,
grumbling not when my day goes wrong,
there to relax me from the human throng,
moist black nose, nestled 'gainst my cheek,
what would they ask if they could speak?

Lady, Tommy, Oliver, Pepe and Joe,
I love you more than anyone will know,
you're always there when I need a friend,
to my moaning you listen without end,
so, carry on enjoying your carefree days,
you deserve each one, for your caring ways!

David Brasier

SILENT WORLD

People see blindness
They don't hear deafness
They don't understand
What it means not to hear.

The words of a loved one
Whispered in your ear
The voice of your child
Calling your name.

The sounds of nature
The birds in the trees
The wind stirring the leaves
And the patter of rain on the earth.

No one knows what
It's like not to hear
Only those who have lost
This precious gift from God.

Anne Gatehouse

INCONVENIENCE!

Everyone knows the hassle,
The inconvenience of having a cold!
The stuffed up nose, catarrh blocked ears,
Eyes stream and you feel old!

The senses, taken for granted,
We rely on every week;
And then, the toast's on fire
You couldn't smell . . . your nose is weak!

The family's speech is muffled
You can't tell what they say,
It really is frustrating!
'Wish this cold would go away'

Then suddenly you realise . . .
With really grateful mind,
It's really not forever,
Our normal life is kind!

Think then, of the people
Who live in silent worlds,
Who *never* hear what's going on
in conversational whirls

Their friend and true companion,
The dog, who is their 'ears'
Is wonderful . . . and yet is still
Second best to one who hears!

Shirley Williamson

PUPPY TALE

I sit down in the kitchen, and wait
Until I hear a noise at the gate,
Or else hear a sound at the front door,
These are two noises I cannot ignore.

The telephone rings, my ears prick up,
I really am an amazing pup,
Knowing what to do without being told,
Makes me really worth my weight in gold.

The milkman calls, I'm up in a flash,
You'd never think I could make such a dash,
My feet go skittering down the hall,
But I take care, I daren't have a fall.

Me and my master get on so well,
My paw on his knee is needed to tell
When someone has come to visit and talk,
Then sometimes we all go out for a walk.

I am his ears and proud to be here,
I'll help and guide him all through the year,
A touch here, a nudge there, he knows what I mean,
When we're together, we go like a dream.

I had to have lots of training I fear,
To be a pup with a listening ear,
It's hard work I know, but I am so keen,
I'll be the best 'listening ear' dog you've seen.

Isobel Crumley

THE PRISONER

Self-pity saps my energy; I plead
My cause with gathering dismay,
Last-hour hope withering away;
There is so little, yet so much I need

Far distant whisper - be it song-bird call?
Floating memory cannot repeat
The perfection of a paean so sweet,
The most arresting melody of all.

Shackled to my fast receding dream
I frequent a realm, my very own;
Banished to a strange, unfriendly zone
I wonder at providential scheme

That is my lot, hard to understand
So agonising to accept
Making me painfully inept,
Lonely spirit in an alien land.

But the horrific blasting from the mass,
So detrimental to repose
To a more robust region goes;
For me, intangible impressions pass.

Like windows wide my seeing does reveal
The magic of my Lord's design
A Master hand is guiding mine,
He who appreciates my hurt is real

Harbours me, clutching my soul like a sign,
Resignation ripe for His word,
Somehow ethereally heard.
Wonder transforms the prison that's mine.

Ruth Daviat

SMELLY DOG!

I've really had an awful day, though it started
like a dream,
She took me running in the woods so I could let
off steam.
I snuffled off to chase a ball she threw far
through the trees,
Then we sat upon our fallen log and shared
some bread and cheese.
The sun was high and shining, the sky was
baby blue,
I had a quiet chuckle when water
filled her shoe.
I splashed and waded in the brook, and
had a lot of fun,
Then we turned and headed back for home
Too tired now to run.
We stopped to have a natter with a friendly
local poodle,
Then joy of joys, I had a roll in some
gorgeous foxes' doodle!
The sun went in, the clouds came out, my
owner held her nose,
I don't know what was wrong with her,
I smelt better than a rose!
Banished to the carport I heard the
dreadful sound,
Of water filling up the bath and swirling
all around.
She plunged me in the water, and
soaped me up, not nice.
With disgusting smelling dog shampoo,
She even did it twice!
She rinsed me with the shower, I couldn't
have been wetter,
Then I shook myself all over her, which
made me feel much better.

I'm sulking on the hearthrug now,
I'm going to make her suffer,
The very least that she could do is give
me extra supper!
Tomorrow when we're out again, and she's
resting on our log,
I'm going to go and leap right in
a lovely smelly bog!

Judith Christie

JOURNEY'S END

'Why did you pick such a moth-eaten hound?'
'And where's his collar and lead?'
'Whatever made you go to the pound?'
'I really don't know,' I said.

'You don't even know what his parents are,
or what kind of life he's led'
'And why are his feet all covered in tar?'
'I really don't know,' I said.

'Why is his coat so coarse to the touch?'
'Looks like he's never been fed.'
'And why is it you that he loves so much?'
'I really don't know,' I said.

'But I know how he'll be in a few days from now,
After he's watered and fed,
With a place by my side on the living room couch,
He'll be beautiful then!' I said.

'I know that he's kind and he's clever and smart,
Not where he was born or was bred.
His new place now is deep down in my heart,
We'll never be lonely!' I said.

Beryl M Truman

A Thousand Words

To write a thousand words would not describe your loss,
of this special person, who meant the world to you,
Resentment, guilt, bitterness, but through your grief
a new you emerges, to face once again your life,
A mixture of emotions are a thousand words,
Where are we, what are we doing, where are we going,
Ask and you will receive and just believe, the
good book says.
How many times have you prayed, for the
strength and courage to fortify and multiply
your belief.
In your thoughts you twist and turn, to help
and retrieve and surely learn, the thousand words
Do not leave me, please help, the outstretched hand
is given, but no one answers, so alone, I am living,
just living.

Margaret Gibson

WHAT WAS THAT?

Did you hear a little noise?
Was it something meant for me?
I saw your ears suddenly twitch
I cannot hear you see
Was it someone passing
Or the click of the latch on the gate?
Are you awaiting a knock on the door
As your reaction I await?
You are a faithful little friend
You alert me to every sound
Life has been much better
Since you have been around
What would I do without you?
I cannot cope alone
I am sure you know you are doing good
As my love for you has grown
You never ask for any reward
Just the pat of my hand
I know when you look with your loving eyes
That you understand
We get along together
I cuddle and hold you near
You are always ready and willing to work
You know I cannot hear.

Evelyn Evans

UNTITLED

If I could not hear
Would miss the sound of
raindrops pouring on the waves
Horses' hooves clip clopping on gravel
dogs barking at dawn
the snowflakes on trees
the sound of rattling snakes
birds singing music at dawn
the sound of waves on the rocks
herons swooping and splashing.

Kheenah Fossey (6)

UNTITLED

If I could not hear
I would miss the sound of
The bird tweeting in the tree next door
The calm sea splashing on rocks
The leaves in autumn rustling
In summer the gate next door clanging
Dad playing downstairs
Mum doing the washing outside my room
The door closing downstairs.

John Sparrow (7)

UNTITLED

If I could not hear I would miss the sound of
the birds singing in the morning
my teacher
people singing at school
people talking
the rain
my best friend
the waves against the rock
the wind
fish swimming
the music
people playing.

Lydia Nero (6)

UNTITLED

If I could not hear
I would miss the sound of
Birds singing in the treetops.
Leaves rustling in the wind.
Church bells ringing in the morning.
The soft music playing in my room.
My friend singing in the garden.
My cat miaowing in the kitchen.
People talking in the park.
The telephone ringing in the bedroom.

Catherine Wilkins (6)

IN PRAISE OF HEARING DOGS!

Yours is a dog who earns his keep
Doesn't forget or oversleep!
Always alert and very bright
Keeping his owner's needs in sight.

Very happy to be with you
Answers your needs, as is your due,
Bright as a button, trained with care
So overjoyed to do his share.

Fun you will have, company too
Security for both of you.
A welcome home, a friend indeed
A normal lifestyle you can lead.

What could be better? Who can say,
Enjoy each other every day.
These special dogs, so good and kind
Bring lots of love and peace of mind.

Jean Howell

TOBY

(A poem dedicated to a rescued mongrel and much loved pet)

I went for a walk along the shore,
I watched the restless sea.
My best friend gambolled and played nearby,
My dog always comes with me.

We watched the birds out on the wet sand,
And heard their tuneful song.
A stick is dropped at my feet to throw,
My dog always comes along.

Back home, it's time for tea and cakes,
A snack for me to eat.
But who could resist those pleading eyes,
As he asks, 'Where is my treat?'

An evening in front of the TV set,
My favourite shows to see.
I would knit as well to pass the time,
But he's lying on my knee!

It's time for bed and I climb the stairs,
Weary and ready for sleep.
But a black, hairy angel is snoring away.
Toby, dream on, at my feet.

Val Cole

HEARING DOGS FOR THE DEAF

Right since birth I've been slightly deaf
But was always full of life,
hospitals were my favourite place -
I took everything in my stride.

Many 'ops' on ENT I had
My name was very well-known,
The nurses were *all* my favourites,
I was never in fear, or alone.

Old technology had rarely worked,
so when I married I 'let things be',
But my ears just went from bad to worse,
More help was needed, I had to agree.

More trips to hospital once again,
My surgeon this time, Mr Evans.
With my neglect, the infection was rife,
he took one look and exclaimed 'Good Heavens!'

In two weeks' time I had a bed,
for an 'op' to repair perforation,
But tiny internal organs I had
put paid to that creation!

Consent wasn't needed first time around,
but now I would have to 'sign'.
'The 'tools' are too big to get inside,
I'll go through the back - you'll be fine!'

The 'op' a success, with a new skin graft,
and my head all bound up like a 'mummy',
My husband came in with request of my camera -
The resulting sight was real funny!

A year or two later, the other ear's turn,
but by then there were more new ideas.
A substance called 'Jellafoam' was placed inside,
Closing the hole, without pain or fears.

Job's done, my hearing improved with the time,
The surgeon said 'Don't use an Aid,'
But at favourite shows I missed words and rhyme
so dismissed his advice, all the same.

I now have a posh and private pair
to help me along life's way,
But to them I'm becoming beholden,
I just hope I don't rue the day!

But 'God Bless' him, all the same.

Lynne Cotton

IN HONOUR OF FAVOUR

Don't know much about puppyhood
I don't know who really cared
About me when I was a puppy
Or whose home it was I shared.

I just remember being lonely
And scavenged dustbins galore,
Being caught and taken to kennels.
Oh! My life was such a bore.

Then one day, two faces through the wires
Glanced down at my skinny frame,
They seemed to be liking what they saw,
Perhaps 'twas for me they came.

My brown eyes pleaded, I cocked my head
And hoped they would understand,
How much I wanted someone to love
To be stroked by a caring hand.

We played some games with a squeaky toy
And some other sounds they tried.
They seemed surprised when I gave a paw.
Then they took me for a ride.

Two other dogs were there to greet me,
Sam and Anna were their names.
I didn't lose my love for dustbins.
'Twas for me such fun and games.

I heard folk say that I was special,
The first of many, they said.
As a mongrel I gained admittance
To Crufts - 'For the highly bred'.

I toured for miles with my master,
Gave demonstrations galore.
I mixed with the elite on telly,
My life no longer a bore.

In the newspapers I was featured,
And magazines as well.
For my job was indeed a 'special'
As the deaf people will tell.

For them it's a world full of silence,
And for some a world of tears.
So a dog like me who has been trained
Can replace their deafened ears.

Somewhere in this my lifelong story
Is a lesson to be learned.
Now I hear my master's voice saying
'Favour' your retirement you've earned.

Thank you so much my master, dearly,
For the love and patience shown,
I feel that we have learned together
As the seeds of time have grown.

Your favourite Favour.

June Ironside

TAMSIN THE TV KID

The alarm has gone off, it's 6.30 in the morning
Next to my bed, something's stretching and yawning
A paw reaches out from a cosy arm chair
And with a thud it lands on my hair!

I open my eyes and before me I see
Tamsin, The TV Kid - my border collie!
The TV Kid, she earned her name
By 'Dobbing the Knob' on the telly - a great game!

Eyes glued - you'd think it was a sheep!
She thinks this is how to earn her keep
But to me, this obsession's a small price to pay
For the love that she shows me, unconditional each day!

Michelle Perry

THE SILENT SHORE

One of life's great pleasures
Has always been for me
Just to stand and listen
To the ever surging sea.

I sometimes sit and wonder
How lonely it must be
To be so isolated
From the music of the sea.

To see the constant motion
Of the waves against the shore.
Never hearing nature's symphony
That goes on for evermore.

To see the little children
Being happy at their play,
To see their bright eyes shining
But miss everything they say.

We hear the seagulls screaming
And complain of the nuisance
But if the deaf could hear them
They would get right up and dance.

B C Watts

BODY LANGUAGE

Hello! My name is Sulla and I'm two and a half years old
For a little black poodle I'm very smart, or so I have been told.
I think my Dad is deaf you know
But when you look at him it doesn't show.
When my Mum is not around
He doesn't react to every sound.
To gain his attention a bark's no good
So I tap his knee, or give him a shove.
But the best thing I've found to get him on his feet
Whether it's a tiddle I need or something to eat,
Is to wag my tail and give him a lick
Then he says 'What's up Sulla?' double quick.
So a bark or a grumble are no advantage
But we get on a treat with our body language

Jennie Goodall

MAYBE!

I've never been keen on dogs, so I thought -
until my daughter to us brought
a tiny spaniel she was to train,
if all of us could stand the strain.

A hearing dog, who'd leave his bone
to alert his master to bell or phone,
to sit when told, and do his bidding.
But not our Reeves, you must be kidding.

A run in the park his eyes would plead.
As soon as we'd get there, unclip the lead,
he'd go like the wind, off to the trees
and sniff around for as long as *he* pleased.

There's something exciting under a log,
then he'd spot another dog.
Off he'd race for a rough and tumble
leaving us to fume and grumble.

Will he make it, you well may ask?
Will he really be up to the task?
At the moment he is just a baby,
so the answer now is -

maybe, maybe!

Doris Baker

DOG WISE
(Dedicated to the memory of my dear mother, Lilian Birkbeck)

Dog is God spelt backwards
Just reflect on that
When you push me off your favourite chair
And resign me to the mat.

I'm here to teach a thing or two
To you snarling, snapping men
Who don't appreciate that laws of God
Need keeping, yes all ten!

You see how loving I can be
Despite the slaps and scolds,
I show how it was meant to be
When God made human moulds.

How sad it is the angry brigade
Should rule the roost down here.
Every bitter word or angry jest
Still make Him shed a tear.

With a tail wag, a proffered paw
I make each day a treat.
Now please follow my example
Freely loving those you meet.

With my pert ears I listen well
That's what deaf friends ask of me
And I am a sure-foot guide my dear
For those who cannot see.

So, if I do I like a bit of spoiling
Well, what's the harm in that.
A crunchy bone or chocolate sweets
I'm sure won't make me fat.

So come along now man o' mine
Don't treat me like a rat
'Cos dog is God spelt backwards
Drat, I'd better not chase the cat!

Teresa Tipping

SILENT WORLD

With deafness the world is silent
We know this is not true,
Our hearing dogs provide the loss
Of things we cannot hear, or do.
Life would be empty and lonely,
Not so with our wonderful dogs.
Where would we be without you,
Our faithful working friends.
You are our loving saviours
Each and everyone of you.
Dogs of every size and breed
Help us in our hours of need.
Loving helpful and always there
Our hearing dogs are trained to care.
So thank you for training with care and grace
For our wonderful, companions, we cannot replace.
The love and affection our friends touch and tell
The wonderful hearing dogs, loved as well.

J Winters

WORTH THEIR WEIGHT IN GOLD

Take a stray from off the street,
Give it water and food to eat.

Send it up to Oxon way,
Instruct it kindly - every day.

Take it slowly a bit at a time,
Do it properly in deed and mime.

Teach this dog its new vocation;
Send it to its new location.

Love it, groom it, train it well,
Be it boy dog - be it girl.

Tend it daily, with loving care,
Teach it listen, here and there.

Whistles, ringing bells and crying,
Knockers, phones and baby sighing.

These this dog will quickly learn,
Important things it will discern.

Trained to be the perfect ears,
To give to someone, faithful years.

Unwanted dog? (Shout it from a steeple)
It's now a Hearing Dog For Deaf People!

Joyce Dobson

LOUIS

There you lay on the cold kennel floor
waiting for a new family that you could adore
we gazed into your sorrowful eyes
and knew we had found a wonderful prize.

They said you were old and prone to be sick
were we sure we should make up our minds so quick
but we knew right away we had to adopt you
the offers to re-home you so far, had been few.

We bought lots of toys, a bright collar, a lead
all of things we thought you would need
but it was our love and affection that you really craved
we gave you it all, you were so well behaved.

Your health never good, suddenly began to wane
visits to the vets again and again
we did all we could to make your life long
but by late summer our dearest friend was gone.

Nothing could ever take your place
your beautiful ways your cute happy face
the love for you in hearts will remain
until the time comes till we're with you again.

Tracey Thompson

UNTITLED

In a sea of silence I was drowned,
My only sense was fear
This void to which I now was bound,
Would never disappear.
Once vibrant, in reality
Everything seemed dead.
A black and white existence
Had coloured life in dread.

Hands reaching to touch
The untouchable, so near
But out of reach they clutch
Only emptiness and fear.
Invisible torment,
Dreadful mime
Friendliness rejecter
Wading through time.

But sense returned
The day you came
To ease my burden,
Soothe my pain.
A friend indeed,
A gentle paw,
So real and there
An open door.

Hands reach to touch
The touchable, alive and warm
There to love and give so much
My shelter from that silent storm.
A vibrant world with colours clear
Reveals no mystery now you're here.
On you I know I can depend
My precious dog and treasured friend.

Gillian Lacey

MAN'S BEST FRIEND

She helps us to hear things
Like fire bells and things
Burglar bells
Alarm clocks
And other important things
Man's best friend.

She helps us to do things
Like calls me when the telephone rings
When the doorbell dings
And lots of other important things
Man's best friend.

Louise Granshaw

IF I COULD NOT HEAR

If I could not hear,
I would miss the sound of
The sea singing in the breeze
The trees rustling in the wind
The wind howling in the night
God speaking softly to me
Birds singing at dawn
My best friend's voice down the street
Aeroplanes flying in the deep blue sky
The sound of my pencil when I write.

Gemma Moore (7)

IF I COULD NOT HEAR

If I could not hear I would miss the sound of,
bluebirds singing in the treetops,
bright blue waves crashing on the rock,
my best friend's voice,
the rain dripping on the windowsill,
the soft music at my ballet school,
the singing at the church,
a waterfall crashing into the pink and purple ocean,
fish swishing in the blue-green lake.

Verity Handyside (7)

MY BOYS

Just over ten years ago, I went to Battersea
We wandered round the dogs' home, my boyfriend Noel and me.

After many hours and floods of tears, I saw the 'perfect' pair
They were, they said 'a handful', but I really didn't care.

Once papers signed, donation paid, we took hold of their leads
And headed back for Ealing with our two scruffy crossbreeds.

They came not without problems and could sometimes be so bad
And in those very early days they often drove me mad.

But once they'd learned they were to stay, they settled in at home
They were well-behaved in every way, even when alone.

My boys, Scruffy and Scramble, had become almost as one
Inseparable at all times bringing and sharing fun.

The years went by, my lifestyle changed and Noel left the scene
But me, Scruffy and Scramble remained a stronghold team.

We moved out to the country which I knew they would adore
With smells to smell and fields to run, which dog could ask for more?

They made new friends day after day, so popular my boys
With pats on heads and treats to eat and loads of squeaky toys.

I hoped it would last forever, but this was not to be
For early on one Saturday, one was taken from me.

It was, they said, impossible as no-one could predict
That he would one day suffer from a long and fatal fit.

To end his pain I let him go, the hardest thing I've done
He seemed so small and helpless, my youngest little one.

Scramble found it very hard, we both just cried and cried
Neither of us understanding why our team member had died.

So now there's just the two of us, my good-old-boy and me
And wherever I go now, he's always there with me.

Of course I know the day will come when Scramble goes to play
With Scruffy wherever he is now - I really dread that day.

But no matter how much hurt and pain that there will surely be
I would not have missed them for the world for they mean
                                                    the world to me

Claire Paine

MY DOG

My dog is a greyhound-Labrador.
When I am not happy she cheers me up.
When I want to play she plays with me in the field.
She is my best friend.

Nicole Hughes (7)

PLEASE JUST LISTEN

I have a profoundly deaf friend and on the way to town one day
we were walking slowly, happily signing as we went along our way.
She was kicking her feet through the leaves that had fallen to the ground
making that wonderful shushing noise but my friend couldn't
                                                        hear a sound.
So I asked her 'Do you know that when you do that the leaves
                                                make a noise?'
She turned and looked at me blankly and almost lost her poise
she thought I was accusing her of being noisy, she's not a noise maker
and the thought that she was being troublesome really seemed
                                                        to shake her.
So she answered me, one of the saddest things that I ever heard
(Deaf people refer to having 'heard' though they cannot hear a word)
'I know the leaves must be silent as they fall down off the trees
by the softness of their movements as they flutter down in the breeze,
so it never crossed my mind that they might be noisy on the earth
I've seen children kicking the leaves and laughing for all
                                                they were worth.'

Can you imagine not knowing that lovely sound made by the
                                        moving of dried leaves
and that anyone might be upset because that person for one
                                        moment believes
that fallen leaves could be noisy and that someone might be offended.
There's no way of describing, without comparisons, and our
                                        conversation ended.
It's impossible to describe that sound to someone who has never heard
that autumn sound of the leaves nor the singing of a bird.
It is said that the sweetest sound, to a widow, would be her
                                        husband snoring.

We all complain of noise but try to imagine being unable to
hear a brook pouring
over the stones and pebbles - to hear children laughing or even
to hear them cry.
All hearing people should give thanks for the gift until the day they die.

Florence Broomfield

WELCOME TO MY CANINE FRIEND

I cannot hear a baby cry,
or hear a bluebird sing,
I cannot hear the rain that falls,
or Sunday church bells ring
    But I can see the babies smile
    and see the bluebird fly,
    and I can feel the gentle rain
    that falls from God's blue sky.
I've never heard a babbling brook,
or heard the thunder roar,
I cannot hear the mighty waves,
come crashing on the shore.

I never hear the ticking, of the old grandfather clock,
Never have I heard, a friendly postman's knock.

    Mine is a silent, silent world,
    but what joy, came my way,
    into my silent, silent world,
     The day you came to stay.

Jacqueline Claire Davies

SHADOWY HOUND

Damp and still the trees remained
In Cannock Wood, and full of mist,
Silent, save for pattering rain
And sounds so mute, too often missed.

My shadowy hound, one with the night,
Came and went among the trees,
His path betrayed, though out of sight,
By chink of name tag, slush of leaves.

I stood and listened, heard a sigh
Faint as the breeze in pine tree bough -
Sense alert to the faintest cry -
No more did ear or eye allow.

With crunch of gravel, on we trod,
The track defined, though black with peat -
No sight but trunks in mouldering sod,
No sound but mine and scuffling feet.

No pangs of fear, no demons felt.
The wood is nature's, God's and ours.
The forest ride, the pine tang smelt
Showed in the dark the salient power.

The stillness touched me with an ease -
I felt that God has brushed my side,
The way I sensed my dog, unseen,
Yet in the hush, a quiet guide.

L A Rosenberg

REMEMBERING BUSY 'BONNIE'

When dear old Patch died,
We thought our hearts would break,
But when you arrived, Bonnie,
You helped to ease the ache.

The last of the litter,
One eye brown, one eye blue,
As soon as we saw you,
No other would do.

Little did we know,
What a character you'd be
Always making us laugh,
And such good company.

A true border collie,
How you loved to manoeuvre
All kinds of things
But, particularly, the hoover.

With jobs finished inside,
Then out you would go,
To give assistance to John,
Who was starting to mow.

How you prodded that mower,
You didn't lack nerve,
And the lines on the lawn,
Took on a slight curve.

When out in the garden,
You were always insistent
That when holes needed digging
You were our chief assistant.

And how you loved TV
Snooker was your favourite
And didn't you run
When we shouted, 'Here's Steve Davis.'

Always so lively
Like a bottle of fizz
Your nickname, inevitably,
Became Billy Wizz.

The years went so quickly
Just where did they go?
Our dear Billy Wizz
Has become Billy Slow.

Such an effort to walk
Such an effort to breathe
The vet said, 'I'm sorry,
Just a matter of weeks.'

It hurt so much to lose you
Our Bonnie, more than a pet,
They say 'You'll love another,'
We say 'Not yet, not yet.'

Susan Reilly

THE STORY OF MONIQUE

When I went to the Home, back in March, '83,
'Twas a pitiful sight to behold, you'll agree.
At the back of a cage, all alone and forlorn,
Sat a little black dog, wond'ring why she'd been born.

But the kennel maid brought her outside, on a rope,
And the look in her eyes seemed to say 'There's still hope!'
As we went to the car, she jumped in with delight,
Thinking 'Someone, at least, was aware of my plight!'

When we entered the house, she admired the settee,
Took a jump and lay down, and said 'Now where's my tea?'
I was shocked and I stared, and remarked 'What a cheek!
You'd have thought she'd been here for the whole of the week!'

But her hair grew so quickly, it hung down in locks,
As she ransacked the house and demolished my socks.
By and by, she became more mature in her ways,
And her loyalty merited nothing but praise!

As the years flitted by, she grew handsome and strong,
And we walked many miles - the whole island along!
She was featured in books, and became quite renowned,
Once a mis'rable waif, now a beautiful hound!

'If the Birmingham Home rescues dogs such as me,
I will do what I can to support it and see,
If, by climbing a mountain, good folk I inspire
To donate needed funds, then I'll climb till I tire!'

Now, her word was her bond, and she climbed to the crest
Of the mighty Ben Nevis, with scarcely a rest!
And the people responded and gave what they could,
And the venture resulted in nothing but good!

All the dogs in the Home gave a 'Woof' of applause,
When the news filtered through, and they offered their paws
To the folk looking round for a pet, somewhat rare.
. . . But a dog is a dog, and they *all* need our care!

Noel Blackham

GLENNIE

Glennie is a special boy,
a standard poodle, not a toy.
His handsome looks change every day,
from posh dog look to scruffy mutt.
He steals your heart, loves you, but
he is a special lad indeed.
He is my 'ears' when I'm in need.
We go to work at night and day,
his role to him is really play.
He tells me when the patient's come,
if the phone rings - is it Mum?
Chemical mixers, smoke alarms,
all the patients Glennie charms.
Bleeps and buzzers, to him they're fun,
the doctor's paper delivered at a run.
We work in x-ray, did you know?
You'll meet us there if you have to go.

Margaret Tovey

MY HEARING DOG

Now I have a hearing dog we'll have lots of fun.
We'll ride on buses, trains and trams,
we'll cross the sea to see my son.
We'll play ball on the beach and splash in the sea
when we have finished we'll go home for tea.
We'll visit all cafes, hotels and the shops,
what a change in life for me, such wonderful company.
He can hear the telephone, he can hear the door,
he is so clever this I know, you do not need to tell me so.
How I love my hearing dog and he loves me,
now I think there is nothing else we need.
He puts on a yellow coat for all to see,
he is there to see to me such wonderful company.

Monica Saunders

AU-PAIR OF EARS

'My-Ears'
have such appealing eyes
that catch my sight
when baby cries . . .
Should my phone ring
then My-Ears
present their-nose
'the-little-dears' . . .
But, you know
there's even more . . .
they sleep upon
my bedroom floor
and if there's need
and 'smoke' should show
my eager-ears
will let me know . . .
Then when the clock
alarms to wake
my faithful-ears
make no-mistake . . .
A gentle-nudge
from well-trained-paws
alerts my ears
and 'open-doors' . . .

Barry Howard

THE GUARDIAN
(My Rottweiller - Bronson)

With powerful jaws - a man's leg wide -
He waits, impressive, by my side.
Against my frame, waist high he stands.
His paws are wider than my hands.
With barrel chest stuck proudly out,
My protector he, so have no doubt.
Crowds may part as we pass by,
He surveys our path with cautious eye.
But once at home, on familiar ground,
A change in his demeanour, found;
My guardian reverts to type;
Bad press about him, media hype.
He frolics 'round the lounge and hall
Searching wildly for his favourite ball.
He lays his huge head on my knee,
His pleading eyes gaze up at me
For biscuits or for chocolate treats -
My guardian loves boiled sweets.
He snuggles by my feet at night,
His sleeping bulk, a soothing sight.
From threats and menace he will defend,
But he's a gentle giant, and he's my friend.

J A Clarke

A Co-operative Success

Your child is partially deaf he said
On our startled unbelieving ears
His words fell as lead raindrops
As we held back the tears.

She will never hear or speak correctly
Hammering home our worst fears
This starched white coat drones on
As we held back the tears.

That was over four years ago
When a group of people resolved
To work in union with a single aim
Her disability to be solved.

So many a visit to hospital
With portage at home each day
Audiology, ENT and Speech Therapy
All pulling in the same way.

Then came a day a year ago
What wondrous a sight to see
Elizabeth with special hearing aids
Listening to birds in a tree.

Later came a jumble of words
Now her world is so sunny
No longer did we hold back the tears
When Elizabeth said 'Mummy.'

So this is just one tiny story
Yet more than gold is its worth
How people are working together
For the good of all on this earth.

D A Watson

TOUCH AND TELL

I'm a lucky young dog called Nell.
I'm lucky because I can tell
When folk at the door ring the bell.
I hear alarm clocks and timers full well.

I hear when the telephone rings
And lots of other things.

The lady I live with can see
But she's not really lucky like me.
The trouble is she cannot hear
That's why she likes having me near.

She knows that I'll hear every sound
And to her side quickly I'll bound.
I'll alert her at once with my paw
And lead her to phone, clock or door
Or cooker and she'll do what's right
To meet the occasion, day or night.

I'm proud to do this for my friend
And glad that my ears I can lend
To make her life happy and much more secure.
Of this I'm very certainly sure
We look after each other so very well
I'm happy and proud to be *Hearing Dog Nell.*

E D Parrott

FARM DOGS

Milky and Dairy
Were dogs on the farm
They kept pigs in their pens
And they kept the cows calm
They followed the farmer
All over the fields
Rounding the sheep up
For their daily meals.

At the end of the day
When all jobs are done
They are given their dinner
And snooze in the sun
The cats wash their faces
The hens seek their nests
But Milky and Dairy
Have earned their nice rest.

Vicky Kingsnorth (13)

What? Pardon? Can You Say That Again?

I know it's difficult for you to understand
why I get depressed the way I do,
but I want to help you to understand
so try and see it from my point of view.

I make everyone's life more difficult
and I drive you all insane,
by answering all your questions
with 'What?', 'Pardon?', 'Can you say that again?'

I'm often staring, lost in thought,
thinking 'Why me?' 'What did I ever do?'
But it's a question no one can answer.
It didn't have to be me, it could just as easily have been you.

Still you've all helped me with my problems
and I hope I've helped you with yours.
But I don't need advice now, I need support,
because one day I may not hear you anymore.

Sarah Louise Burslem

SILENCE

Though silence may be golden
To those of use who hear
Its constance can be scary
On the deaf - it causes fear.

The telephone, a doorbell
An alarm - to be alert
With deafness there's no difference
So someone could be hurt.

Imagine total silence
Where not a sound is heard
No whizzing by of traffic
Or singing of a bird.

Where men about construction work
Are smiled at - never frowned
For to those who cannot hear them
They never make a sound.

A banging door, a barking dog,
A baby full of screams
For those who live in silence
Their noise is only dreams.

So when hearers next seek silence
Let's question - why the need
For those who live it daily
Seek the power to be freed.

Pauline Foran

DOGS

Dogs can give us company,
They can tell when we are sad
So try to make us happy.
They can be our best friend:
There for us when no one else is,
Helping us not to be lonely.
Dogs are very comforting
And their warm bodies comfort us
When we are scared and insecure.

Dogs can give us hours of fun
With their affectionate ways
And happy, playful nature.
If we are lucky and have dogs,
We know what good friends they can be.
We could never be without them
And the warm softness of their fur.
Dogs aren't just stupid animals,
They're loving and caring
And always there for us.

Victoria Knight (13)

IN MEMORY OF MY THREE PRECIOUS STRAYS

The twilight of his life has now begun
How hard it is to take now that time has come
Some time has passed since I began to write
And now that twilight has turned into night.
He lies relaxed, asleep. He will not wake
Only a few will know of the heartbreak.
My vet throughout the years was very kind
But now I must put sadness all behind
And think of all the happiness he gave
Companionship and love. I was his slave
The holidays, the walks, romps in the grass
And now he sleeps beside my Mick and Lass.
Two other precious pets that I once had
The three of them, their lives had been so bad
Poor Lassie with her feet so red and raw
And Mickey, well he just lay at death's door.
Chippie survived that dreadful dreadful flood
But after all that there was only good
And after all the misery they had had
They must have thought - well this is not too bad
I don't think I can go through this again
With all the tears - the heartbreak, all the pain
But somewhere in the future there may be
Another little dog in need of me
A little stray may come my way and then
I'll set off on that heartbreak course again.

Peggy Edwards

NEW DOG

Your face lit up when us you saw
Standing outside your kennel door
Your eyes were begging, take me home
Don't leave me here all on my own

Your coat was shiny your nose so wet
The friendliest dog we'd so far met
You stood there all skin and bone
We knew we had to take you home

At first you emptied out the bins
And chewed up all sorts of things
You dug holes in the garden and grass
But thankfully those times have passed

You've now settled into your new home
No more are you all skin and bone
But a healthy, cuddly, contented boy
Happy with his new-found joy.

Sue Starling

JESS

Whatever did I do without her? you ask.
Well - not a lot.
Not since my old man died,
And there I was, on my own,
Without a sound.
No phone, no doorbell, no voices to cheer me.
Oh, I got all the gadgets,
And got used to them - eventually.
But they were dead things.
How I missed my dear old man!

Then Jess came -
Jess came, with her cold wet nose, her persistent paw,
Her fun, her friendship,
And her love.
Oh no, she's not just *useful,*
She's not just my *ears* -
She takes me for walks, she makes new friends,
She makes me laugh.
She's not just a *dog,* you know -
She's given me the world,
She's given me life.

Mora Hawkins

POPPY

Run free my darling Poppy
Away from all your pain
The hurt is ours to suffer now
Will life be the same again?

You shared our lives so briefly
Then we had to say goodbye
Just two short years is all you had
And how time rushes by

You brought such joy into our lives
In those happy sunlit days
And enchanted everyone you met
With your sweet and gentle ways

We tried so hard to make you well
In every way we knew
But sadly in our task we failed
And had to face the truth

I didn't want to say goodbye
But your suffering hurt me more
And in my arms you found the peace
To suffer pain no more

The house is very still now
And the walks are not much fun
How I long to hold you once again
Or watch you as you run

Sleep well my darling Poppy
We're so sorry that you've gone
You'll stay in my heart forever
Your memory lingers on.

Lynne Churchyard

On Puppy Socialising

How can you bear
To give them back
It's what everybody says
To part with them
When you have learned
Their special little ways

It's not for me
I could not part
With a dog I'd grown fond of
You must be hard
To give them back
After weeks and weeks of love

No - I'm not hard
I shed a tear
Each time a pup's returned
It is a wrench
To turn your back
On love you have not earned

But think of this
Each dog you help
Could be a person's ears
Become their friend
Stay at their side
Help take away their fears.

You have a chance
To help someone
You may never even meet
By being kind
And putting up
With two pairs of muddy feet.

Joyce Kingman

MY DOG

Are you listening
My old obedient friend?
I remember you panting
Right up to the end.

Your eyes grew dim
There was no bark
You were very thin
Now you're in the dark.

At the end of the tunnel
You will see a bright light
Where you'll run and howl
For the rest of your life.

No this is not the end
We shall meet again
Up there in heaven
You and me, old friend.

Bill Thomson

HEARING DOG FOR A DEAF FRIEND

At the beginning of my life
I was passed around like a dice
Always felt unwanted and alone
Oh no, another new home.

I have never asked for much
Just a little love and such
How I long for the changes to end
to allow my broken heart to mend.

What a surprise I had this morning
I was unaware a great day was dawning
A lady came to visit me
She was nice, I sat on her knee.

The lady took me for a walk
When we got back she had a quick talk
Then I got into her large van
A long journey to my new home began.

I soon settled down
Once I'd looked around
It wasn't long before I did some training
During which my confidence was gaining.

Then came the day when I met my new mother
We got on well and liked one another
Then I got my certificate to say
I am a 'Hearing Dog' and here I will stay.

Sarah Meakins

Hear, Hear

My old Grandad used to shout,
'What are you boys whispering about?'
That was because he couldn't hear,
Unless you shouted into his ear.

He never complained about our noise,
When we were boisterous young boys.
So I suppose there's some consolation,
In being deaf in that situation.

We all loved to visit our Grandad,
Because although we usually went mad,
He just sat in his old rocking chair,
Smoking his pipe and polluting the air.

As a young man he had volunteered,
To defend the country where he was reared.
He was deafened by the cannonade,
And returned home needing a hearing aid.

He never received any compensation
From the 'supposed to be grateful' nation.
Because all the money was needed for,
The country to prepare for another war.

He always cupped one ear in his hand,
When he listened to Jimmy Shand.
And he drank his wee dram neat,
As he swayed to the stirring beat.

At his wake many a tear was shed,
For the old warrior who now lay dead.
And I hope to St Peter, he won't shout,
'Young man, what are you whispering about?'

Thomas Boyle

JACKIE (A TRUE STORY)

I remember the first time I saw him
a crippled starving stray
Hanging around outside our home on Famagusta Bay
His sad brown eyes looked up at me, eyes which
seemed to say, I just want someone to love me
so please don't send me away.
We really didn't want a dog - that wasn't
in our plan
But there he was, and so you see that's how
it all began.
He became a constant companion, he joined
in all our fun, walking and swimming
and sailing, or just lying in the sun.
Years of love and devotion he gave us - we
hoped it would never end - but one sad
day it happened, we lost our faithful friend.
He's in his doggy heaven now and we are
here alone,
I wonder if he thinks of us as he chews
his celestial bone.

Irene Roberts

My Harry

Harry looks up lovingly
His furry face a frown
'Are you going out today Mum
Will you leave me on my own?'

I bend and scoop him in my arms
'To the shops I have to go
I promise you I won't be long
I'll be back before you know.'

Harry's not a 'hearing dog'
But seems to know so well
I do not hear the phone ring
Or the sound of the doorbell.

He jumps and barks and leads me there
Though, we never taught him to
As if he's trying to tell me
'I do this just for you.'

One day I'll have a 'hearing dog'
But until that moment comes
I'll stick with my little Harry
He and I are best of chums!

Liz Scrivens

BOSUN'S BATHTIME

'I wonder where my Mum has gone,
Wherever can she be?
She's not in the garden,
I've looked in the loo
And it's nearly time for my tea.

Oh! Here comes the bucket and the bath
The jug and saucepans too.
Now I know
Where she was
And *what* she's going to do.

Here she comes in 'mac and wellies'
An apron too I see,
A brolly now
Is all she needs
Oh! Why do this to me!

They say it's all for my own good
And my coat is getting better
My head and shoulders
Have improved
Right now I'm getting wetter.

At last it's done, a good rub down
A shake or two from me.
I'm sure I look
As handsome now
As that 'fella' on TV.

Bosun Preece!

HEARING DOG NICK

Little Nick
Every trick
Touch and tell
Does it well
Everywhere
Here and there
And even too
When I'm on the loo!
Doesn't hesitate
(I just can't meditate)
Got to go
He told me so.

John V Roberts

SEEING IS BELIEVING

I like to sit here in the summer
I come here most every day,
Of course I couldn't make my way at all
If my dog didn't know the way

Oh yes, I see colour quite a bit
It's detailed vision that I lack
To me, you're just a coloured shadow
With the sun behind your back

I have enjoyed your conversation
In many ways I'm rather bright
The good Lord didn't steal my brain
He just took back a little sight

When those Guide dog people told me
That I could share, one of their friends
It was like hearing God apologise!
And try to make amends!

For now I have the whole wide world
A world I thought I'd never see
And though I don't see as well as you
I'm a prisoner set free.

If I could buy a thousand friends
For the thousands just like me
I would train a thousand Guide dogs
And set a thousand prisoners free

But life is governed by the rules
That colour cash book's *red*, or *blue*
And it's only in the minds of fools
That dreams like mine, come true

But if *you* were to tell a dozen friends
Of my foolish little schemes
And if each of them believed the same
That would be the stuff of dreams

The Guide Dog people could, with ease
Turn *my* dreams into yours
And a thousand dogs would be the keys
To open a thousand doors

I can tell that you are leaving now
I could feel the park bench move.
Of course, you can pat my Guide dog
She quite likes you, she'll approve

Oh yes, I've had her many years
And I love her more each day
Of course I think she's beautiful
But, who am I to say?

But, perhaps you'll help me, if you can
Before you go on your way
Tell me Mr Shadow man,

Is she as lovely as they say?

R Hurrell

COCOONED IN LONELINESS

Trapped by a world of silence
I long for yesterday.
I want to share life with you
and hear the things you say,

How much of life I'm missing
cocooned in loneliness,
whilst endless talk and laughter
bring anguish and distress.

I miss the sound of music,
The gentle song of birds.
The joy that's lost forever
I cannot put in words.

The restful running water
and softly rustling breeze.
I'd give the world to capture
the pleasures such as these.

Who understands my sadness
and hears my plaintive cry?
In solitude I linger
and watch the world go by.

Why do you walk away now
and treat me like a fool?
I didn't know that deafness
would be so very cruel!

Let me be a part of things
and live the way you do.
Don't think that I am different
for I am just like you.

John Christopher

ON BEHALF OF A DEAF FRIEND
(Deceased)

I saw the lark ascending
But could not hear her song
I saw the hammer lifted
But did not hear the gong
I saw the boughs a'bending
Away in yonder trees
I do not know the difference
In sound of gale or breeze.

The waves upon the beach-head
Pound high above the wall
They say the sea's a siren witch
I answer not her call
The ballet dancers pirouette
On television show
I do enjoy the spectacle
But music cannot know.

The ringers are at practise
At church on Tuesday night
I'm told they are improving
And Sundays get it right.
And when in congregation
The choir raises voice
I see their faces moving
And watch their lips rejoice.

I thank the Lord for senses
Of sight and touch and smell
But wish that he had blessed me
With ears that work as well.
And when I see the organist
Tune up to notes and clef
I sadly rue my natal day
When I arrived *born-deaf!*

Marion P Webb

A WET NOSE

Wanting weighs me down
Weariness and sadness cling to me like sodden clothes which
can't be cast off.
Fears and doubts follow me like shadows in the dark
Looming larger than they really are.
Undoing me
Haunting me
I call out but self-pity drowns my voice.
Where are you?
Where are you?

No voice calms me
No arms comfort me.
No hands come and wipe away my tears
No lips come and kiss me.
I plead and plead for rest and . . .
And then.
A nose.
A wet nose and a head quietly rest on my knee.
A tail wags
And my dog.
My old old dog comes to me as my Lord.
In meekness and gentleness and love.
I cry.
Again I cry. Slowly.
Warmth and joy cry with me
As the morning breaks and darkness slinks away.
Wanting weights me down
No more.

Lynne Chitty

FOUR-LEGGED FRIEND

Can the rest of us ever imagine
What it must be like
Not to hear the birds sing?

The rain upon the windowpane
The wind amongst the trees
Even the bees.

The things we often complain about
The dripping tap
The telephone ring
Even the television.
All the things we take for granted
If we are able to hear.

But what of people who are not able?
The hearing aid for some is obvious
For some to write a note is needed
I marvel at the sign language
Just to communicate with each other.

But when they're alone at home
Who then to watch and listen?
Thank goodness for their four-legged friend
Trained to help - to be their 'ears'
To give support and confidence
In the things *we* take for granted.

Mary A Slater

PAL

The doorbell rang, 'Pal' was on the alert
With eyes wide open, a wag of the tail
He nudged his mistress who had not heard
And ran to the door to collect the mail.

In came the paper, he laid at her feet,
With abounding joy he returned
To fetch the letter that lay on the mat
For his mistress these things he had learned.

The kettle was whistling for a good cup of tea
And 'Pal' once again did the trick,
Gave her a nudge, to the kitchen did go
Then returned with a wonderful lick.

He heard the gate open, he heard the gate close
'Pal' knew that someone was there
He went to the door, barked once that was all
Of which the milkman was quite well aware.

'Pal' is so faithful he stays by her side
Till a noise gives out the alarm
Then quickly he moves to where the sound comes
Making sure she comes to no harm.

'Pal's' aware that his mistress is deaf
Needing help and guidance in life,
He is always ready and willing
Keeping her out of trouble and strife.

When you're alone and cannot hear
A dog is a faithful friend
Good company, trusting,
To the very end.

Eileen Chamberlain

DIFFERENT

Please don't laugh at me, say I can't play,
Don't say I can't join your group, 'Go away!'
I can't help the way I was born with
My hearing far from the norm.
I cannot help it if I'm not as quick as you
In solving problems in working them through.

Imagine how you'd feel if all the world's sounds
Seem muffled as if from far under the ground.
There are things I can't hear like the rustle
Of leaves or the call of the dove high in the trees.
The tick of the clock as time passes by or the drone
Of a plane high in the sky.

You are lucky your life is perfectly fine,
You can hear what's going on all the time.
But think of all the people like me,
Those who can't hear and those who can't see,
Those who are dumb and those who are lame
Disabled we are called but that's just a name.
We are people like you just different that's all,
Please be our friends, help us walk tall.

M M Hunter

No 435

I had my face washed this morning before I left my bed -
Kim heard my alarm clock and her tongue whisked round my head.
Her feet descended on my chest and then down the stairs she sped.
Breakfast time arriving, on the whistle, eat.
Weigh her breakfast out and use the rest for treats.
Paw on knee 'What is it Kim?' she's lying at my feet.
The smoke alarm's been ringing I've gone and burnt the toast,
Kim gives me a hug which says she loves me most.
Paw on knee 'What is it Kim?' Oh! Now it is the post.
Hanging out the washing standing all alone,
Along comes Kim and touches and takes me to the phone.
It interrupts her nap, but I never see her moan
Now it is lunchtime, but Tony can't be seen,
'Kim call Tony for me please!' I don't know where he's been.
'Hello Tony' Kim brings him back, she's always very keen.
Now where is Kim? I can't see so I'll press the squeaker twice -
She comes bounding up, paw goes on knee, she is here
                                                in just a trice.

Now, you may think she's perfect, and she doesn't have a vice,
But loo rolls are her favourite thing, she's had them by the score.
Woe betide anyone who forgets to shut the toilet door.
She's seen TV the Andrex pup and shreds them on the floor.
Dark brown eyes and dark brown fur, touched in parts with gold.
You should see her face, if I ever have to scold.
Whatever did I do before Kim came to stay?
I know for certain she has brightened my day.
From morn till dusk she's at my side
When she wears her coat out we walk with pride.
Thanks to the sponsors for making this possible,
And the work of the trainers - which always looks impossible.

J Lawrence

DOG

We walk again, new dog and I,
the muddy fields I walked before.
It's not the same I want to cry.

Old canine friend I helped you die
and wept to see you stilled. No more
to walk again, old dog and I.

New dog is young and bright of eye
and makes me miss you even more.
He's not the same I want to cry.

Before you left we said goodbye -
you licked my face, I smoothed your paw.
Can't walk again, old dog and I.

New dog is sleek, new dog is spry.
Just give me time - we'll find rapport
and be the same I want to cry.

He runs, I call; he comes, sits by.
He licks my face, I smooth his paw.
We walk again, new dog and I.
Not quite the same. I want to cry.

André Lewis

MAN'S BEST FRIEND

(Dedicated to 'Patch' and her owner Eric Griffiths)

When I was a child I could hear everything
From a thunderstorm at night to the morning birds singing
But as I grew older the sounds seemed to fade
So an appointment with the doctor I made
From that day forward my life turned around
He told me I was deaf, and then suddenly frowned
There was nothing I could do to prevent it
So I had to handle it bit by bit.
I started off with a hearing aid
But no difference to me it made
So I wrote a letter to Hearing Dogs for Deaf People
They phoned me back, they were very helpful
I waited for two years then I got a letter
They said they had a 'hearing dog' which would make
                                        my life better
I went to the centre and they introduced me to Patch
And then I knew we were a perfect match
Now three months later she's living with me
Thank you Patch for helping me be free.

Cathy Wilson (15)

SHEBA

(Sheba born 9 Sept 1977 saved from further
suffering 17 Feb 1989 - Labrador cross terrier)

As I sit here with you beside me
I think of words, that once were spoken.
That final day decisions were made.
When all our hearts were badly broken.

Since that day, it's been a year.
I think of you and shed a tear.
I miss you girl, I miss you bad.
I feel so empty and ever so sad.

As I think back to those summer days
Of watching you run through those waves.
I think of us walking across golden sands.
At least you're a dog, that cannot be banned.

On the Isle of Colansay, we set you free.
We miss you Sheba, the family and me.

Another year has just gone by
And still I ask the question why
Why oh why did you have to go?
The answer is 'I do not know.'

Sharon Rowe

A FAITHFUL FRIEND

Surrounded in a world of silence
She hears no knock upon the door
Telephone rings do not disturb her
Nor footsteps that walk upon a floor.

Whistling kettles go unnoticed
Fire alarms are never heard
Children calling out in pain
But she doesn't hear their words.

Now suddenly her whole world changes
To all these things she now responds
There is no human walks beside her
But with a hearing friend she has a bond.

No more she misses people calling
This faithful friend will let her know
And in the lonely hours of evening
A little dog's affection shows.

Now her silent life is filled with joy
On someone whom she can depend
And as people go on disappointing
She can always rely on *man's best friend!*

A Lane

MAX

Max is Margaret's wonder boy
Truly he's her pride and joy
His sensitive - sharp - keen - ear
Alerts to what she cannot hear

She's confident in his sensitive touch
He knows she loves him very much
His eyes are beautiful - his coat is warm
She's proud to lead him on her arm.

Love

Max.

Margaret and hd 'Max'

THE ALARM CLOCK IS RINGING

I stretch in my bed;
And look at my mum
The old sleepyhead;
With one bound or two
I land on her bed
She opens her eyes
And fondles my head.
Night is now over,
We start a new day
Such faith in each other
For our work and our play,
My mum cannot hear,
So I am her ears,
I'm rather timid,
Mum calms my fears,
We are such a good team
My mum and me
For I do love my mum,
and I know mum loves me.

'Star' (Hearing Dog 310)

SILENCE IS NOT GOLDEN

Silence is golden,
so the old saying goes.
But take it from me,
as someone who knows.
I can't hear the children,
while laughing at play.
Or the birds singing,
on a warm summer's day.

If silence is golden,
I long for the day
When I hear again
the sound
of music.
The cry of a baby.
The children at play.
Then I would be able to say
Noise!
Not Silence is *Golden!*

Brian Edwards

MOON KISS

Cuddle the moon, kiss a star
Pick this up, you're not that far
You're reading the written lines
Close to your own face
And recalling the times
At a certain place
You may not be able to hear
But like words, God is near
The concentration riding a bike
Deaf, I don't know what it's like
Balance like a lost tear
I still can't imagine no sound
Footprints, noise on the ground
Perhaps it's like the dark space
Where noise is gone without trace
Movements like the rivers
The earth turns the shivers
Even if I put my mind to it
I'll never find sound words to fit.

John A McVey

A LEARNING CURVE

The new dog
Is an old dog
From the rescue centre.

Brown and white,
Fat and furry,
With a plumed tail
And anxious eyes.

He barks incessantly,
Snarls at other dogs,
The clearest commands
Fall on deaf ears.

He breaks through fences,
Tramples the garden,
Digs huge craters.
Must he go back?

Then slowly
His character emerges.
He picks blackberries
From the hedge.

He looks soulful,
Lies in the sun
On his back; we say
'Duke' is in residence.

Ann Hiam

HARD OF HEARING

What? Sorry I am slightly,
Deaf, just one ear,
Yes, that is right, I,
Have had an operation,
But, still cannot hear.

Pretend I am not deaf,
Work in all the,
Jobs, I shouldn't,
Do, until one day,
The Doctor says,
You must rest,
Oh No, I can hear.

I think we all have,
A cross to bear,
Some can cope,
But I live in,
Hope, that one,
Day, I will hear,
In that ear,
One day, What did you say?

B Brown

SILENCE

When I lost my dog Bonnie
Everything in my life changed
In fact that life was no more
and a new one took its place.
No more barks, no whining,
no sniffs, no speaking to her
Just an empty house and silence.

KK

ILK'S SOLILOQUY

I wonder if she's brought any chocolate today
a sly, sidelong glance so not to betray
that despite my sobriety I am at heart a pup
and if you feed me non-stop I should still eat it up!

The first day you took me out I felt extremely sad
you see I didn't know you and I did so miss my dad
reluctant were my pawsteps as you took me to the sea:
I thought 'I'm never going home' what a tragedy.

I am a hard working dog and execute with care
all my canine duties with a serious stable air
but wasn't it a change when you took me to the park
and I somersaulted over and you even heard me bark.

Dependable and faithful I've lived for seven years
yet I do like a cuddle to know that someone cares
it's true I'm rather heavy to imitate a cat
and all that lovely chocolate is making me quite fat.

When I am in harness my behaviour is sublime
so I have to be let off the lead to romp about sometime:
these are the words of Ilk a worthy Labrador
who shows his appreciation by extending his right paw!

Carole Marie Irvine

TISH MEETS THE CANADA GOOSE

Mother Goose and her goslings
Were 'sunning' by the lake
When 'Tish', the dog, got nosy
And liberties did take.

'Tish' edged toward the goslings
A-snuffling as she went,
And Mother Goose, got very cross
Although no harm 'Tish' meant.

Arching her neck, 'Mum' flapped her wings,
Her frantic lunge made 'Tishy' cringe.
Soon, doggie 'Tish' was in retreat,
To safety 'neath the lakeside seat.

Betty E Keeler

A PIECE OF *DOG*GEREL?

The gasman is calling but cannot say when,
So I'll have to spend time by the front door again!
No trips to the garden for washing and that
Or 'sorry, you were out when I called' on the mat.

Now that I have my so sweet golden dog
No more I experience life in a fog,
For Sandy will tell me if anyone's near
Or telephone ringing, all sounds I don't hear.

This dear little creature - (a wonderful cure
For that horrible feeling of 'not being sure')
Gets me chatting to strangers with never a fear,
Something I have missed out on for many a year.

Now it's on with my plimsolls and battered straw hat
For a game of her football - (where *did* she learn that?)
Her habits and mine have now blended so well -
To give thanks to you *all* it's my pleasure to tell.

Meg Weaver

BLOSSOM

Blossom is my hearing dog.
Learning to touch and tell.
She is funny, quick and loving.
Alert from top to tail.
She often flies upstairs.
In response to my call.
Following me from room to room.
My bestest friend of all.

Janet Cook

A HEARING DOG'S PROMISE

I'll be your ears
To stop your fears,
I'll serve you day and night,
I'll be your friend
Until the end,
And love you with all my might.

Carly Turner (7)

WORLD OF SILENCE

In my silent world
A voice from within me cries
Unheard by the world outside
I cannot hear
Nor speak, nor make a sound
And yet a silent inner voice
From deep within me
Cries out aloud
Within my silent world
From which there is no escape
There is no malice
Within my heart
Nor hate against the world outside
For I am blessed
With an inner sense
That others have been denied.

A W Harvey

DEAFNESS

I've learnt a new language,
I hope you will help and understand
No talking to me loudly or, quietly
Or behind the flat of your hand.
No walking past me and talking as you go;
Why? Because I am deaf you know.

No talking to me, with your head drooped
To the table, as you speak.

I have to look at your lips,
To understand the words that you speak.
The music and sounds I enjoyed in days gone bye.

I can't hear now, so have to read
them from your lips,
Please try and help and speak to me clear.
It's so frustrating, when you can't hear.

Joan Patrickson

JACK

When the sounds of life begin to fade
and silence takes its place
it brings an isolation
a fear so hard to face

I miss the sound of loved ones' voices
the words of favourite songs
all the beautiful sounds of nature
I've enjoyed for so so long

but I will not let this beat me
there has to be a way
to regain a quality of life
and communicate each day

so I learnt the art of reading lips
and to sign the words by hand
communication now regained
once more I understand

but life was still not quite complete
there were things I could not see
the doorbell rang a friend would call
or a phone call meant for me

and on a more important note
with safety deep in mind
if the smoke alarm should give the call
that fire would not be kind

once more I felt the panic
the loneliness, the fear
I need that something special
to keep me safe, to hear

it was then I had a lifeline
a hearing dog named Jack
not just a dog, but a special friend
he gave my hearing back

once more those early morning calls
a gentle touch from Jack
I wake to see his smiling face
my independence back

I can't explain the magic
while sitting drinking tea
when I get that gentle touch from jack
it's the telephone for me

and no more my friends must stand and wait
while ringing on my door
it's touch and tell, then come on mum
you have visitors for sure

each night I now sleep peacefully
contented in my bed
for if the fire should start
with Jack to safety I am led

so thank you all at Lewknor
you have given me back my ears
but most of all a friend for life
to guide me through my years.

T N McIntyre

HEARING DOGS

You watch with amazement,
At the things those dogs can do,
and how many deaf people,
Would love to own one too.

It alerts its master or mistress,
That someone's at the door,
Not with a loud barking,
But a tapping with the paw.

The same when baby's crying,
A touch then off to the cot,
That dog was not shifting,
Until someone came to the spot.

But what if an alarm should sound,
The owner has no fear,
The dog would keep on pawing,
To make sure that all got clear.

And when the alarm clock is set,
They can settle for the night,
Knowing that their faithful friend,
Will paw when it is right,

Now all these dogs need training,
But the money must be found,
So that Hearing Dogs for Deaf People,
Can use up every pound.

The training of a Wonder Dog,
Needs patience, time, and skill,
Then their owner gets more freedom.
so with *your help* they will.

Will A Tilyard

THE LOVE WE SHARE

I stroke your smooth black glossy hair,
Your eyes hold that adoring stare,
Yes, I was captured from the start.
You've wound your way into my heart.

Yes you are my very best friend,
I will love you to life's end,
These lovely times we share together,
I'll remember for ever and ever.

Life slows down from that hurried pace,
I feel relaxed, worry leaves my face,
We find peace together you and I,
Worries drift by, they are pie in the sky.

When we've had a snooze, and it's time for tea,
We'll share a cuppa, you and me,
Then a walkies we will go,
My doggy pal, I love you so.

Eileen Handley

MY FAITHFUL FRIEND

D o you realise what a silent world is ours
E rasing every pulse of living sound?
A pealing bell, bird song, a barking hound
F ail to brighten up our lonely hours.
N o one who has their senses all intact
E ver can imagine what we've lost,
S o friendship given at so little cost
S peaks volumes, though not heard. And that's a fact.
A nd looking at my ever faithful friend,
N odding at my feet with one ear pricked
D evotion fills his eyes - 'It's *you* I've picked -
D epend on me, my love will never end.'
O thers round the world have not our joy,
G oing through their lives in deep despair,
S o think of them and show them that you care.

Paddy Jupp

DEAFNESS

To live with deafness,
Ears blank and empty of sound.
Covered since birth.
Voice unheard, unplayed
No sound from man, wife or child.
The mind screaming, shouting.
Ears blank and empty.
But wait, somewhere deep
In recess of the mind
A soundless well of knowing,
A coloured cloth of sound
Woven into patterns
On the canvas of the mind.
And in some unlooked - for morning
The screaming and the shouting stops.

Idris Woodfield

MERLYN

A tiny puppy in a box,
Travelled home from Wales,
So quiet and apprehensive,
As the car ate up the miles.

A glorious liver coat he grew,
So handsome, so debonair,
He sat with his back so very straight,
His nose up in he air.

He ran and jumped, enjoyed his life,
Chasing squirrels, cats and rabbits,
We could not stop him any way,
He got into very bad habits.

he put up with the children,
with Amber, Zak and Gem
He did not once snap or snarl,
Just sighed and turned away from them.

And then the light began to fade,
His eyes grew steadily dimmer,
His coat less shiny and not so dark,
He became a little thinner.

He passed away at Christmas,
To the kennel in the sky,
He'll run and jump and play there too,
Just like the times gone by.

Lea Wright

INFORMATION

We hope you have enjoyed reading this book - and that you will continue to enjoy it in the coming years.

If you like reading and writing poetry drop us a line, or give us a call, and we'll send you a free information pack.

Write to :-
**Triumph House Information
1-2 Wainman Road
Woodston
Peterborough
PE2 7BU
(01733) 230749**